EMMANUEL JOSEPH

The Forgotten Virtues: How Lost Principles Can Restore Humanity in a Digital Age

First edition

This book was professionally typeset on Reedsy.
Find out more at reedsy.com

Contents

1

Chapter 1: Rediscovering Honor

In the annals of history, honor was once the bedrock of personal and societal conduct. It was more than a mere concept; it was a way of life. Ancient civilizations, from the samurai in Japan to the chivalrous knights of medieval Europe, revered honor as a virtue that defined one's character and social standing. These cultures understood that honor was intrinsically linked to integrity, respect, and duty. Upholding honor meant adhering to a code of ethics that transcended personal gain, fostering trust and cohesion within communities. However, as modern society evolved, the clearcut codes of honor have blurred, and the digital revolution has further complicated our understanding and practice of this ageold virtue.

In today's digital age, the anonymity afforded by the internet has significantly altered our interactions. Social media platforms and online forums often mask identities, enabling behaviors that might be avoided in facetoface encounters. This shift has led to a perceived decline in honorable conduct, with cyberbullying, misinformation, and trolling becoming rampant. Despite these challenges, the relevance of honor has not diminished; rather, it has become more crucial. Honor in the digital age involves being truthful, respectful, and accountable, even when shielded by a screen. It requires a commitment to ethical behavior and respect for others, reminding us that our actions, online or offline, have realworld consequences.

To reintegrate honor into our digital lives, we must begin with selfawareness and education. Practically speaking, this means fostering digital literacy that emphasizes the importance of ethical behavior online. We should promote and practice transparency, ensuring that our digital actions reflect our true values. Encouraging accountability in online communities can also help; implementing systems where users must own their actions can deter dishonorable behavior. Furthermore, by highlighting and rewarding examples of honorable conduct online, we can create a culture that values and upholds this virtue. In essence, rediscovering honor in the digital age is not about returning to the past but about adapting timeless principles to contemporary challenges, ensuring that honor remains a guiding star in our collective digital journey.

2

Chapter 2: The Power of Empathy

Empathy, the ability to understand and share the feelings of others, is the cornerstone of human connection. From an evolutionary standpoint, empathy has been vital for survival, fostering cooperation and strengthening social bonds. Research in neuroscience has identified mirror neurons as key players in empathetic responses, allowing us to "mirror" the emotions of others, creating a shared emotional experience. This biological underpinning highlights that empathy is hardwired into our brains, emphasizing its fundamental role in human interactions.

Despite its importance, empathy seems to be dwindling in the digital age. The rise of digital communication has created a paradox; while we are more connected than ever, these connections often lack depth. Text messages, emails, and social media posts can strip away the nuances of facetoface interaction, making it harder to convey and perceive emotions. The physical distance and anonymity provided by digital platforms can desensitize us to the impact of our words and actions on others, leading to a decrease in empathetic behavior. Studies have shown a decline in empathy among younger generations, who are growing up immersed in this digital environment.

However, all is not lost. We can nurture empathy even in a digital world by making conscious efforts to deepen our connections. One approach is to engage in active listening, truly paying attention to others' words and emotions. Another is to use video calls instead of textbased communication, as seeing each other's faces can enhance emotional understanding. Encouraging open and honest conversations about feelings and experiences can also foster empathy. Additionally, digital platforms can be used to share stories that promote empathy by highlighting diverse perspectives and experiences. By making these small yet significant changes, we can build stronger, more compassionate communities in both our online and offline lives.

3

Chapter 3: Integrity in a Transparent World

Integrity forms the bedrock of trust and ethical behavior, embodying honesty, consistency, and strong moral principles. Historically, integrity has been pivotal in both personal relationships and societal structures, shaping the ethical framework within which individuals and communities operate. It entails doing the right thing, even when no one is watching, and maintaining consistency between one's values and actions. As a timeless virtue, integrity has upheld the pillars of justice and fairness, ensuring that actions are aligned with ethical standards and social responsibility.

In the digital age, the landscape of integrity is challenged by the unprecedented transparency and interconnectedness of our lives. Social media platforms, blogs, and digital footprints lay our actions bare for the world to see, often subjecting them to public scrutiny. This visibility can tempt individuals to curate dishonest portrayals of themselves, seeking approval and admiration at the expense of authenticity. Additionally, the anonymity provided by digital interactions can erode accountability, leading to behaviors that diverge from one's true values. The rapid spread of misinformation, fake news, and cyber deceit further complicate the practice of integrity in an online environment that sometimes rewards sensationalism over truth.

To maintain and promote integrity in this transparent world, several strategies can be employed. First, selfreflection and continuous ethical education are paramount; understanding and defining personal values helps anchor one's actions. Embracing authenticity in digital interactions, resisting the urge to present false narratives, and prioritizing honest communication foster genuine connections and trust. Implementing and supporting systems that enhance transparency and accountability, such as verified identities and ethical guidelines for online conduct, can deter dishonest behavior. Finally, leading by example and acknowledging the impacts of one's digital actions encourage a culture of integrity that can inspire others to uphold ethical standards. By integrating these practices, we can navigate the complexities of the digital age while preserving the timeless virtue of integrity.

4

Chapter 4: Reviving Patience in an Instant World

In the current era where instant gratification reigns supreme, patience has become a rare virtue. The pervasive presence of technology offers us immediate solutions and instant results, often leaving little room for the slower pace that patience demands. Despite the convenience of this fastpaced world, the benefits of patience remain invaluable. Practicing patience reduces stress, improves decisionmaking, and fosters resilience. It enables us to appreciate the journey rather than just the destination, contributing to a more balanced and fulfilling life.

The impact of patience extends beyond individual wellbeing to our personal and professional relationships. In personal interactions, patience allows us to listen more deeply, understand others' perspectives, and respond thoughtfully rather than react impulsively. It nurtures empathy and strengthens bonds, as it shows that we value and respect the time and feelings of others. In professional settings, patience is equally crucial. It aids in strategic thinking, enhances teamwork, and improves problemsolving by allowing us to approach challenges with a calm and focused mindset. By practicing patience, we build trust and credibility, fostering a positive and productive work environment.

Cultivating patience in a fastpaced world requires intentional effort and practice. One effective strategy is mindfulness meditation, which trains the mind to remain present and focused, reducing the urge for immediate results. Another approach is to set realistic expectations and break tasks into manageable steps, allowing for a more measured and patient progress. Additionally, practicing gratitude helps shift our focus from what we lack to what we have, fostering a more patient and content outlook. By integrating these practices into our daily routines, we can revive the virtue of patience, enhancing our wellbeing and enriching our relationships in both personal and professional spheres.

5

Chapter 5: Humility in the Age of SelfPromotion

In an era where social media platforms often glorify selfpromotion, humility stands out as a vital yet understated virtue. Humility involves recognizing our limitations and valuing others' contributions without seeking constant recognition or applause. It fosters a sense of groundedness and authenticity, promoting genuine connections over superficial acclaim. Historically, humility has been lauded by philosophers and spiritual leaders as essential for personal growth and societal harmony. It allows us to learn from our experiences and from those around us, fostering an environment of mutual respect and continuous improvement.

The digital age, however, presents unique challenges to maintaining humility. The pervasive culture of online validation can lead to arrogance, as individuals constantly curate and share their most favorable moments to garner likes, shares, and comments. This focus on selfpromotion can breed a sense of superiority and entitlement, eroding genuine interactions and selfawareness. Arrogance, in turn, can alienate others and create unrealistic expectations, ultimately leading to dissatisfaction and a lack of meaningful connections. The constant comparison with others' highlight reels can also foster insecurity, as individuals feel pressured to meet unattainable standards.

To stay grounded in a world of digital accolades, it is crucial to practice humility intentionally. One effective approach is to regularly engage in selfreflection, assessing our actions and motivations. This practice helps us remain true to our values and recognize the contributions of others. Additionally, limiting time spent on social media and focusing on facetoface interactions can help foster deeper, more authentic connections. Celebrating others' successes and expressing gratitude for their efforts also nurtures a culture of humility. By incorporating these practices into our daily lives, we can navigate the digital age with a balanced perspective, valuing humility as a timeless virtue that enhances our personal and communal wellbeing.

6

Chapter 6: Courage in the Face of Digital Challenges

In the vast landscape of the digital world, anonymity often emboldens negative behavior. Hidden behind screens, individuals may express harmful comments or engage in cyberbullying without facing immediate consequences. This environment can create a breeding ground for dishonesty and cruelty. However, digital courage serves as a powerful antidote. Digital courage involves the bravery to uphold integrity, stand up against harmful actions, and foster positivity, even when it is easier to remain silent or join the crowd. It requires a conscious effort to promote kindness, truth, and justice, leveraging the anonymity of the internet to amplify good rather than conceal malice.

Standing up for what is right in the digital realm is crucial for building a healthy online culture. This can range from calling out misinformation to defending someone who is being unfairly targeted. Exercising digital courage helps to set a precedent that harmful behavior will not be tolerated. When individuals take a stand, they inspire others to follow suit, creating a ripple effect of positive action. It is essential to approach these situations with respect and constructive dialogue, aiming to educate rather than antagonize.

By doing so, we not only protect those who are vulnerable but also contribute to a culture of accountability and empathy.

Fostering a brave and respectful online culture requires collective effort and practical steps. Promoting digital literacy and ethical guidelines can empower individuals to navigate the online space responsibly. Encouraging open dialogue about the impact of online behavior and the importance of digital courage can shift norms and expectations. Additionally, platforms can implement features that support positive interactions, such as reporting mechanisms and community guidelines that prioritize safety and respect. By embracing digital courage, we can transform the virtual world into a space where integrity and compassion thrive, creating a more supportive and inclusive environment for all.

Chapter 7: The Role of Gratitude in Digital Relationships

Gratitude, the act of recognizing and appreciating the positives in our lives, has profound effects on our wellbeing. Studies in psychology and neuroscience reveal that practicing gratitude activates brain regions associated with reward, thus promoting feelings of pleasure and contentment. Regularly expressing gratitude can reduce stress, increase happiness, and improve overall mental health. By focusing on what we are thankful for, we shift our attention away from negative experiences and foster a more positive outlook on life.

In the realm of digital communication, gratitude plays a crucial role in building and maintaining relationships. A simple thankyou message or a thoughtful comment on social media can go a long way in strengthening bonds and creating a sense of connection. Gratitude in digital interactions helps bridge the emotional gap often created by physical distance, making virtual exchanges more meaningful and sincere. It fosters a culture of appreciation and mutual respect, enhancing the quality of our online relationships and communities.

Practicing thankfulness in a techdriven world requires conscious effort. One effective method is to incorporate gratitude into daily digital routines, such as sending messages of appreciation to friends and colleagues or publicly acknowledging the contributions of others on social platforms. Additionally, maintaining a digital gratitude journal where we note down positive experiences and interactions can help reinforce the habit of thankfulness. By embracing these practices, we can harness the power of gratitude to enhance our digital relationships, creating a more supportive and positive online environment.

8

Chapter 8: Wisdom in the Age of Information Overload

In today's digital era, we are inundated with information from countless sources. This constant barrage can overwhelm our ability to discern meaningful content from noise. Cultivating wisdom becomes essential in navigating this landscape. Wisdom involves the judicious application of knowledge, guided by experience and sound judgment. It requires the ability to filter through vast amounts of data, identifying what is credible, relevant, and useful. By developing critical thinking skills, we can better evaluate information, question assumptions, and make informed decisions that align with our values and goals.

Critical thinking is the backbone of wisdom, empowering us to analyze information logically and objectively. It entails questioning the validity of sources, recognizing biases, and assessing the reliability of evidence. In an age where misinformation and fake news are rampant, honing critical thinking skills is crucial for distinguishing fact from fiction. Educational systems and digital platforms can play a pivotal role in fostering these skills, encouraging individuals to engage in thoughtful reflection and skepticism. By prioritizing critical thinking, we can navigate the information overload with greater clarity and confidence.

Seeking truth amidst the digital noise also involves embracing humility and openmindedness. Recognizing that we do not have all the answers allows us to remain curious and receptive to new perspectives. Engaging with diverse viewpoints and acknowledging the limits of our knowledge fosters a more comprehensive understanding of complex issues. Additionally, practicing digital mindfulness—being aware of our information consumption habits and setting boundaries—helps maintain a balanced and focused approach to learning. By integrating these principles, we can cultivate wisdom that not only enriches our personal lives but also contributes to a more informed and discerning society.

9

Chapter 9: Compassion Across Digital Divides

In our interconnected world, compassion acts as a powerful bridge that spans the divides created by differing backgrounds, beliefs, and experiences. Compassion involves recognizing the suffering of others and taking action to alleviate it. It transcends sympathy by compelling us to reach out and support those in need. The significance of compassion lies in its ability to foster genuine human connections, build mutual respect, and create a sense of unity. In a time where digital interactions often replace facetoface communication, the need for compassion has never been greater. It serves as the foundation for understanding and empathy, enabling us to navigate the complexities of diverse online communities.

However, expressing compassion in digital interactions presents unique challenges. The absence of physical cues such as tone, facial expressions, and body language can lead to misunderstandings and misinterpretations. Additionally, the anonymity of the internet can sometimes desensitize individuals to the impact of their words and actions, resulting in a lack of empathy. The fastpaced nature of online communication can also encourage superficial exchanges, hindering the deep connections that compassion requires. Despite these obstacles, it is crucial to cultivate and demonstrate compassion in our digital engagements to maintain the human touch in our interactions.

To foster empathy and understanding across diverse online communities, we can adopt several strategies. Firstly, practicing active listening by truly paying attention to others' words and perspectives can help bridge gaps and foster meaningful connections. Encouraging open and respectful dialogue, even when opinions differ, promotes a culture of empathy and respect. Highlighting and sharing stories that showcase diverse experiences can also enhance our understanding of different perspectives. Lastly, leading by example and showing kindness and consideration in our digital interactions can inspire others to do the same. By integrating these practices, we can create a more compassionate digital world that values empathy and understanding across all divides.

10

Chapter 10: Practicing Forgiveness in a Judgmental Society

In a world where people often rush to judgment, forgiveness stands as a powerful and transformative tool. Forgiveness goes beyond simply letting go of grudges; it involves a conscious decision to release feelings of resentment and embrace a mindset of understanding and compassion. This process of forgiveness benefits both the forgiver and the forgiven, fostering emotional healing, reducing stress, and improving overall wellbeing. By choosing to forgive, we open ourselves to reconciliation and create space for growth and positive change in our relationships.

In the digital realm, conflicts and misunderstandings can escalate quickly due to the impersonal nature of online communication. The absence of physical presence and nonverbal cues can lead to misinterpretations and amplify negative emotions. In such an environment, practicing forgiveness becomes even more crucial. It allows individuals to address conflicts with empathy, seeking resolution rather than retaliation. Forgiveness in digital interactions involves acknowledging the hurt, extending an olive branch, and moving forward without harboring ill will. By promoting forgiveness, we can mitigate the toxic effects of online disputes and foster a more supportive and respectful digital community.

To cultivate a forgiving online environment, it is essential to adopt practices that encourage understanding and empathy. One approach is to engage in open and honest dialogue when conflicts arise, addressing issues directly and respectfully. Encouraging a culture of accountability, where individuals take responsibility for their actions and apologize when necessary, can also facilitate forgiveness. Additionally, promoting positive online behavior, such as expressing gratitude and celebrating others' successes, can create a more compassionate atmosphere. By integrating these practices into our digital interactions, we can move past grudges and build a more forgiving and harmonious online world.

11

Chapter 11: Loyalty in a Fluid Digital Era

Loyalty, the steadfast commitment to support and uphold relationships, is a cornerstone of trust and stability. Traditionally, loyalty was deeply ingrained in familial, social, and professional bonds, serving as a bedrock for mutual respect and collaboration. It involves a sense of allegiance and dedication, often requiring sacrifice and prioritization of others' needs. The foundations of loyalty are built on trust, integrity, and a shared sense of purpose, creating resilient and enduring connections. Throughout history, loyalty has been celebrated as a virtue that fortifies relationships and fosters a sense of belonging and security.

In today's fluid digital era, the relevance of loyalty remains significant, albeit challenged by the transient nature of online interactions. The digital landscape often encourages a fleeting approach to relationships, with connections formed and dissolved rapidly. However, loyalty retains its value as it provides continuity and trust in an otherwise fastpaced environment. In professional settings, loyalty to colleagues and organizations fosters teamwork, enhances productivity, and builds a supportive work culture. In personal relationships, loyalty strengthens bonds, promotes emotional security, and nurtures deeper connections. Even in the realm of social media, loyalty to communities and causes can drive positive change and foster a sense of unity.

Nurturing loyal relationships both online and offline requires intentional efforts and consistent actions. One effective strategy is to practice active engagement, showing genuine interest and support for others' endeavors. Communicating openly and honestly helps build trust and ensures that relationships are grounded in authenticity. Additionally, maintaining reliability by following through on commitments and being present during challenging times reinforces loyalty. Expressing appreciation and gratitude for others' contributions further strengthens bonds and cultivates a culture of loyalty. By integrating these practices, we can navigate the fluid digital era with a steadfast sense of loyalty, enriching our relationships and creating a stable foundation for personal and communal growth.

12

Chapter 12: Building a Legacy of Virtue

The ultimate goal of embodying virtues like honor, empathy, and integrity is to leave a lasting legacy for future generations. This legacy is not built overnight but through consistent actions and a commitment to living by these principles daily. Embodying virtues means internalizing them to the point where they become a natural part of our behavior. By practicing honor, we demonstrate respect and honesty in all our dealings, earning the trust and admiration of those around us. Empathy allows us to connect deeply with others, understanding their experiences and emotions, which fosters a supportive and compassionate community. Integrity ensures that our actions align with our values, creating a sense of authenticity and reliability in our interactions.

Inspiring others to adopt these virtues requires leading by example. When we live virtuously, we become role models for those around us, showing the positive impact that these principles can have on our lives and relationships. Sharing stories and experiences that highlight the benefits of living by these virtues can motivate others to follow suit. It's also important to encourage open discussions about the challenges and rewards of maintaining these virtues, creating a supportive environment where everyone feels empowered to strive for ethical living. Recognizing and celebrating acts of honor, empathy, and integrity within our communities can further reinforce the importance of these values.

Ensuring that these principles endure in the digital age involves leveraging technology to promote and preserve them. Digital platforms can be used to share positive stories, educate others about the importance of virtues, and create communities dedicated to ethical living. Encouraging respectful and honest communication online helps build a culture of integrity and empathy in digital spaces. By setting ethical guidelines and holding ourselves accountable, we can create a digital environment that upholds these values. Ultimately, by embodying virtues and inspiring others, we can build a legacy that transcends generations, ensuring that the principles of honor, empathy, and integrity remain a guiding force in both the physical and digital worlds.

The Forgotten Virtues: How Lost Principles Can Restore Humanity in a Digital Age

In a world where technology reigns and digital interactions often overshadow human connections, the timeless virtues that once defined our societies are gradually fading into obscurity. "The Forgotten Virtues: How Lost Principles Can Restore Humanity in a Digital Age" is a profound exploration of how ancient virtues like honor, empathy, integrity, and more can reclaim their rightful place in our lives.

This book delves into the heart of virtues that have guided humanity for centuries, offering a fresh perspective on their relevance in our rapidly evolving digital world. Each chapter intricately weaves historical insights with modernday applications, painting a vivid picture of how these principles can bring balance, meaning, and ethical clarity to our techdriven existence.

Through practical advice, reallife examples, and reflective exercises, readers are invited to embark on a journey of selfdiscovery and personal growth. From cultivating patience amidst the chaos of instant gratification to practicing humility in a culture of selfpromotion, this book provides a roadmap for living virtuously in today's interconnected world.

"The Forgotten Virtues" is not just a guidebook; it's a call to action. It challenges us to rise above the noise, to embrace values that transcend time, and to leave a legacy of virtue for future generations. Whether you seek to enhance your personal relationships, navigate professional challenges with integrity, or simply find a deeper sense of purpose, this book offers the wisdom and inspiration to help you thrive ethically and compassionately in the digital age.

13

Chapter 13: Explanatory on the book: The Forgotten Virtues: How Lost Principles Can Restore Humanity in a Digital Age

Introduction

In an era where technological advancements dominate every facet of our lives, the timeless virtues that once defined humanity seem to be fading into the background. "The Forgotten Virtues: How Lost Principles Can Restore Humanity in a Digital Age" is a profound exploration of how ancient values like honor, empathy, integrity, patience, humility, courage, gratitude, wisdom, compassion, forgiveness, and loyalty can be revitalized to guide us through the complexities of modern life. This book delves into the historical significance of these virtues, their relevance today, and practical advice for integrating them into our daily interactions, both online and offline.

Chapter 1: Rediscovering Honor

Honor was once the bedrock of personal and societal conduct, revered by ancient civilizations for its role in defining character and social standing. This chapter explores the historical importance of honor, from the samurai in Japan to the knights of medieval Europe, and how it fostered trust and cohesion within communities. In today's digital age, the anonymity afforded by the internet has altered our interactions, often leading to a decline in honorable conduct. This chapter offers practical steps to reintegrate honor into our digital lives, emphasizing the need for truthfulness, respect, and accountability online.

Chapter 2: The Power of Empathy

Empathy, the ability to understand and share the feelings of others, is the cornerstone of human connection. This chapter delves into the science of empathy, highlighting the role of mirror neurons in creating shared emotional experiences. Despite its dwindling presence in the digital age, empathy remains crucial for building stronger, more compassionate communities. The chapter explores practical ways to nurture empathy, such as engaging in active listening and using video calls to enhance emotional understanding, fostering deeper connections in both our online and offline interactions.

Chapter 3: Integrity in a Transparent World

Integrity, the embodiment of honesty and strong moral principles, is more crucial than ever in a world where our lives are increasingly on display. This chapter examines the foundations of integrity and the challenges posed by the digital landscape, where transparency can tempt individuals to present dishonest portrayals of themselves. It offers strategies for maintaining integrity online, such as practicing selfreflection, embracing authenticity, and supporting systems that enhance transparency and accountability, ensuring that our actions align with our values.

Chapter 4: Reviving Patience in an Instant World

In an era of instant gratification, patience is often overlooked. This chapter discusses the benefits of patience, such as reduced stress and improved decisionmaking, and its impact on personal and professional relationships. It provides practical advice for cultivating patience, including mindfulness meditation, setting realistic expectations, and practicing gratitude. By integrating these practices, we can revive this vital virtue and enhance our wellbeing in a fastpaced world.

Chapter 5: Humility in the Age of SelfPromotion

Social media often glorifies selfpromotion, but humility remains a vital virtue. This chapter highlights the value of humility, contrasting it with the dangers of arrogance in the digital age. It offers practical strategies for staying grounded, such as engaging in selfreflection, limiting time on social media, and celebrating others' successes. By practicing humility, we can foster genuine connections and create a culture of mutual respect and authenticity.

Chapter 6: Courage in the Face of Digital Challenges

Digital anonymity can embolden negative behavior, but courage is the antidote. This chapter explores the importance of digital courage, standing up for what is right, and fostering a brave and respectful online culture. It discusses the challenges of maintaining integrity in the digital realm and provides practical advice for promoting positive interactions, such as engaging in open dialogue, supporting ethical guidelines, and encouraging accountability.

Chapter 7: The Role of Gratitude in Digital Relationships

Gratitude enhances wellbeing and strengthens relationships. This chapter delves into the science of gratitude, its role in digital communication, and how to practice thankfulness in a techdriven world. It offers practical strategies for incorporating gratitude into daily digital routines, such as sending messages of appreciation, maintaining a digital gratitude journal, and publicly acknowledging others' contributions. By embracing gratitude, we can create a more supportive and positive online environment.

Chapter 8: Wisdom in the Age of Information Overload

With endless information at our fingertips, discernment is key. This chapter explores the cultivation of wisdom, critical thinking, and the importance of seeking truth amidst the noise of the digital age. It discusses the role of critical thinking in evaluating information and offers practical advice for developing these skills, such as engaging in thoughtful reflection, questioning assumptions, and embracing digital mindfulness.

Chapter 9: Compassion Across Digital Divides

In a connected yet divided world, compassion bridges gaps. This chapter discusses the significance of compassion, its challenges in digital interactions, and ways to foster empathy and understanding across diverse online communities. It offers practical strategies for promoting compassion, such as practicing active listening, encouraging respectful dialogue, and sharing stories that showcase diverse perspectives.

Chapter 10: Practicing Forgiveness in a Judgmental Society

In a culture quick to judge, forgiveness is a powerful tool. This chapter examines the power of forgiveness, its role in digital conflicts, and how to move past grudges to cultivate a more forgiving online environment. It provides practical advice for practicing forgiveness, such as engaging in open dialogue, promoting accountability, and encouraging positive online behavior.

Chapter 11: Loyalty in a Fluid Digital Era

L oyalty builds trust and stability, even in a transient digital age. This chapter explores the foundations of loyalty, its relevance today, and how to nurture loyal relationships both online and offline. It offers practical strategies for maintaining loyalty, such as practicing active engagement, communicating openly, and expressing appreciation for others' contributions.

Chapter 12: Building a Legacy of Virtue

Ultimately, the goal is to leave a legacy of virtue for future generations. This final chapter offers practical advice on embodying these virtues, inspiring others, and ensuring that the principles of honor, empathy, and integrity endure in the digital age. It discusses the importance of leading by example, sharing stories that highlight the benefits of living virtuously, and leveraging technology to promote and preserve these values.

Conclusion

"The Forgotten Virtues: How Lost Principles Can Restore Humanity in a Digital Age" is not just a guidebook; it is a call to action. It challenges us to rise above the noise, to embrace values that transcend time, and to leave a legacy of virtue for future generations. By blending historical insights with contemporary applications, this book serves as a timeless guide for ethical living, encouraging readers to embody these virtues and create a more compassionate and connected world.